First Facts®

Snakes

Cobras

by Van Wallach

Consultant:
Robert T. Mason, PhD
Professor of Zoology
J.C. Braly Curator of Vertebrates
Oregon State University, Corvallis

Capstone
press®

Mankato, Minnesota

First Facts is published by Capstone Press,
151 Good Counsel Drive, P.O. Box 669, Mankato, Minnesota 56002.
www.capstonepress.com

Library of Congress Cataloging-in-Publication Data
Wallach, V. (Van)
    Cobras / by Van Wallach.
    p. cm. — (First facts. Snakes)
    Includes bibliographic references and index.
    Summary: "A brief introduction to cobras, including their habitat, food, and life
cycle" — Provided by publisher.
    ISBN-13: 978-1-4296-1923-3 (hardcover)
    ISBN-10: 1-4296-1923-6 (hardcover)
    1. Cobras — Juvenile literature. I. Title. II. Series.
QL666.O64W35 2009
597.96'42 — dc22   2007052038

Editorial Credits
Lori Shores, editor; Ted Williams, designer and illustrator; Danielle Ceminsky,
    illustrator; Jo Miller, photo researcher

Photo Credits
Alamy/Indiapicture/Sharad Bhandhari, 10
Bruce Coleman Inc./Daniel J. Lyons, 17; Dhritiman Mukherjee, 21; Joe McDonald, 20;
    John Shaw, 5; Lynn M. Stone, 12
Getty Images Inc./Gallo Images/Heinrich van den Berg, 7
iStockphoto/John Pitcher, 1
Minden Pictures/Stephen Dalton, 11
Nature Picture Library/Robert Valentic, cover
Pete Carmichael, 14
Peter Arnold/R. Andrew Odum, 19
Shutterstock/Nahimoff, background texture (throughout)
Visuals Unlimited/Joe McDonald, 8–9, 13

Essential content terms are **bold** and are defined on the bottom of the page where they first appear.

1 2 3 4 5 6 13 12 11 10 09 08

Table of Contents

A Dangerous Snake

Cobras are some of the world's most dangerous snakes. They are feared around the world because of their deadly bite. One bite from a king cobra can kill an elephant!

All snakes are covered with **scales**, but not all snakes look alike. Most cobras are black or brown. They can also be red, orange, or yellow.

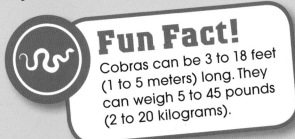

Fun Fact!
Cobras can be 3 to 18 feet (1 to 5 meters) long. They can weigh 5 to 45 pounds (2 to 20 kilograms).

scales: small pieces of hard skin

Home Hot Home

Cobras live in hot areas like Africa and southern Asia. Some cobras live near water. They can also be found in villages where there are rats to eat.

Cobra Range

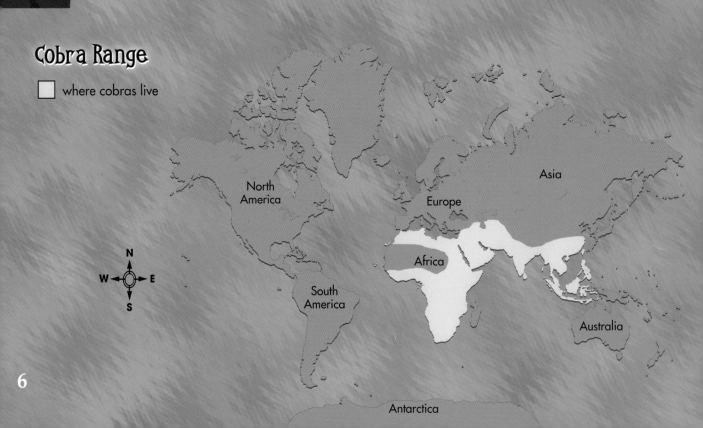

☐ where cobras live

North America

Europe

Asia

Africa

South America

Australia

Antarctica

N
W   E
S

Cobras like it hot because they are **cold-blooded** reptiles. Their body temperature changes with the air and ground around them. When it's cold, cobras lie in sunshine to warm up.

hood

A Scary Show

Most of the time, a cobra looks like any other snake. But not when it is trapped! A cobra can put on a scary show. First the snake stands up tall. Then it makes a loud hiss. Long neck ribs stick out to the side to make a hood. If all else fails, some cobras roll over and play dead.

An Amazing Mouth

Like other snakes, cobras can taste and "smell" with their forked tongues. A special organ in the roof of their mouths identifies the scents.

Cobras are deadly because of the **venom** in their bites. Cobras have two hollow teeth called fangs. Venom flows through the fangs when the cobra bites.

venom: a harmful liquid produced by some animals

Fun Fact!
Some cobras spit venom at an enemy's eyes. They can spit as far as 10 feet (3 meters).

On the Menu

Cobras will eat any animal that fits in their mouths. Frogs and toads are their favorite foods. They also eat reptiles, birds, and small mammals.

Fun Fact!
King cobras only eat other snakes!

Cobras are master hunters. They move quietly in the dark night, searching for **prey**. Then they surprise their prey with lightning fast strikes.

prey: an animal hunted by another animal for food

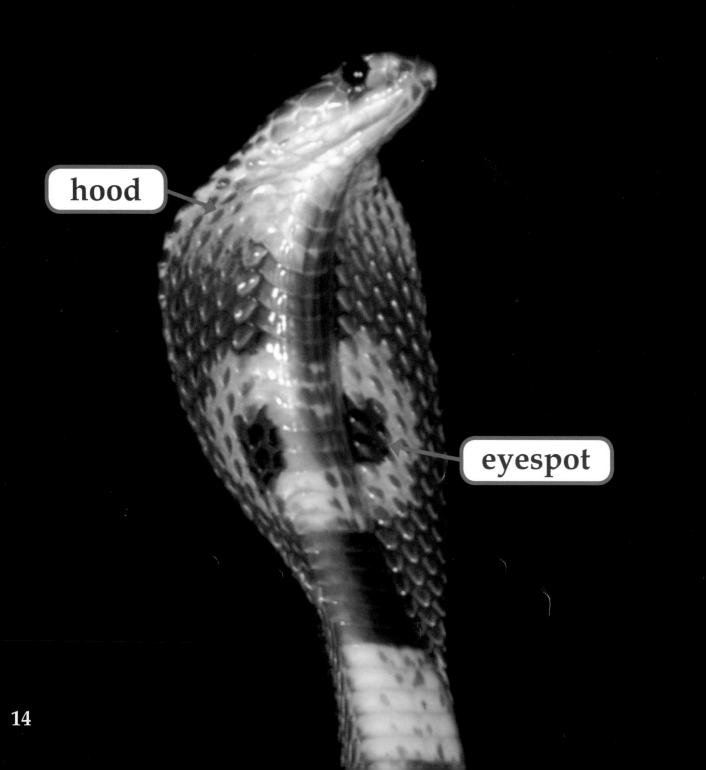

hood

eyespot

Seeing Is Believing

Many cobras have markings on the back of their hoods. Others have spots on the front. Some scientists call these markings false eyespots. **Predators** might think these spots are large eyes. This makes the cobra's head look bigger, which may scare away predators.

Fun Fact!
In many places it is illeg
to keep a cobra as a pe
They are too dangerous

predator: an animal that hunts another animal for food

Family Matters

Male and female cobras mate in the spring. After two to three months, the female lays a **clutch** of 10 to 20 eggs. Most mother snakes leave after laying their eggs. The king cobra is different. It makes a nest out of bamboo leaves. Then both parents guard the nest until the eggs hatch.

Fun Fact!
Snake eggs are oval and white, but they are not hard like chicken eggs. They are soft like leather.

clutch: a group of eggs laid by one female

Growing Up

Baby cobras are ready to leave their eggs in 60 to 70 days. First they peek out of their shells and duck back in. After one or two days, they crawl out.

Young cobras have plenty of strong venom and can hunt right away. At first they eat small animals. As they grow, they are able to catch and eat bigger prey.

Fun Fact!
Cobras continue growing throughout their lives.

Life Cycle of a Cobra

Newborn
Cobras are only 8 to 16 inches (20 to 41 centimeters) long at birth.

Young
Young cobras can double their length in one year.

Adult
Cobras are ready to mate in two to three years.

Newborn

Good Bluffers

Cobras spread out their hoods to scare people away. Cobras are afraid of people. They do not want to bite them. Instead, cobras save their strong venom for catching food.

Amazing but True!

The Choto Pashla village in India is home to 6,000 people and 3,000 cobras! The cobras live in fields and near houses. Villagers worship the cobras and offer them milk. When the snakes die, they are put in pots and placed in the Ganges River.

Glossary

clutch (KLUHCH) — a group of eggs laid by a single female

cold-blooded (KOLD BLUH-id) — having a body temperature that changes with the surroundings

predator (PREH-duh-tor) — an animal that hunts other animals for food

prey (PRAY) — an animal hunted by another animal for food

scale (SKALE) — one of the small pieces of hard skin that cover the body of a fish, snake or other reptile

venom (VEN-uhm) — a harmful liquid produced by some animals

Read More

O'Hare, Ted. *Cobras.* Amazing Snakes. Vero Beach, Fla.: Rourke, 2005.

Spilsbury, Louise and Richard Spilsbury. *Watching Cobras in Asia.* Wild World. Chicago: Heinemann, 2006.

Wallach, Van. *Uncover a Cobra!* San Diego: Silver Dolphin Books, 2005.

Internet Sites

FactHound offers a safe, fun way to find Internet sites related to this book. All of the sites on FactHound have been researched by our staff.

Here's how:
1. Visit *www.facthound.com*
2. Choose your grade level.
3. Type in this book ID **1429619236** for age-appropriate sites. You may also browse subjects by clicking on letters, or by clicking on pictures and words.
4. Click on the **Fetch It** button.

FactHound will fetch the best sites for you!

Index